High-Interest/Low-Readability Nonfiction

Strange and Unexplained

by Kathryn Wheeler

Carson-Dellosa Publishing Company, Inc.
Greensboro, North Carolina

Credits

Editor:
Ashley Anderson

Layout Design:
Van Harris

Inside Illustrations:
Donald O'Connor

Cover Design:
Annette Hollister-Papp
Peggy Jackson

Cover Illustration:
Tara Tavonatti

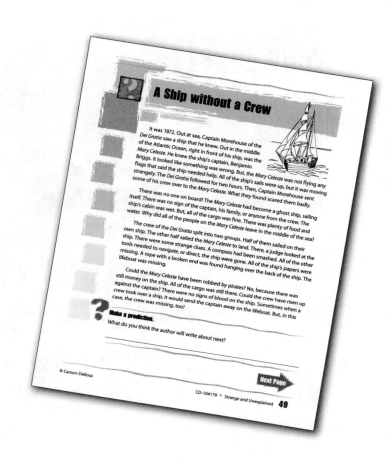

ISBN 1-59441-317-7

Table of Contents

Introduction

Struggling readers in the upper-elementary and middle grades face a difficult challenge. While many of their peers are reading fluently, they are still working to acquire vocabulary and comprehension skills. They face a labyrinth of standardized tests, which can be a nightmare for struggling readers. And, they face another major difficulty—the challenge of remaining engaged and interested while working to improve reading skills.

High-Interest/Low-Readability Nonfiction: Strange and Unexplained can help! All of the articles in this book are written at a fourth-grade reading level with an interest level from grade 4 to adult.

Throughout the book, the stories use repeated vocabulary to help students acquire and practice new words. The stories are crafted to grab students' attention while honing specific reading skills, such as uncovering author's purpose; defining vocabulary; making predictions; and identifying details, synonyms, antonyms, and figures of speech. Most of the comprehension questions parallel standardized-test formats so that students can become familiar with the structure without the pressure of a testing situation. And, the articles even utilize the familiar "Next Page" arrows and "Stop" signs seen in most standardized tests. The questions also include short-answer formats for writing practice.

Best of all, this book will build confidence in students as they learn that reading is fun, enjoyable, and fascinating!

Note: Stories that include measurements, such as a weight or distance, also feature a convenient conversion box with measurements rounded to the nearest hundredth. Students will find this useful as they become familiar with converting standard and metric measurements. If students are not currently studying measurement conversion, simply instruct them to ignore the box. Or, cover it when making copies of a story.

What Was That?!

Imagine you are sitting in your home. You are watching TV. Suddenly, the building shakes. There's a huge noise, like something exploded. When you go outside to look, you find that a huge piece of ice has crashed into your roof!

In 1990, this happened to a family in the state of West Virginia in the United States. A giant block of ice fell from the sky and crashed into their satellite dish! It was two feet long and 18 inches wide. It weighed 50 pounds. All around it were other pieces of ice. Some pieces were the size of baseballs.

The weather that day was clear. The "ice bomb" was not made of hail. The ice had not spilled from an airplane. Scientists knew this because it was just water—there were no chemicals in it. No one could say where the ice bomb came from.

Scientists can't explain the many other reported ice bombs either. One man in the state of New Jersey found a 70-pound block of ice in his house. It had crashed through the roof of his kitchen. In Germany, a worker on a rooftop was hit by an ice bomb that was six feet wide.

There have even been whole showers of ice bombs. This happened in Spain in 2000. Even though Spain is known for its hot weather, big chunks of ice started to fall on towns across the country. In one city, eight ice bombs hit a street in the middle of the afternoon. Another ice-bomb "shower" took place in Colombia. In this fall of ice bombs, an entire village lost their houses. Crops in the fields were crushed.

Are the ice bombs from outer space? Are they parts of an exploded moon or comet? Or, is there a simpler answer to this strange series of events? So far, scientists cannot tell us anything about the ice-bomb mystery.

Conversions

2 feet = 0.61 meters
18 inches = 45.72 centimeters
50 pounds = 22.68 kilograms
70 pounds = 31.75 kilograms
6 feet = 1.83 meters

Next Page

What Was That?!

Answer the questions below.

1. The story tells about ice bombs in all of the following places EXCEPT—
   a. West Virginia.
   b. New York.
   c. Spain.
   d. Germany.

2. Read the following sentence from the story and answer the question.

   The weather that day was clear.

   Which of the following is *clear* weather?
   a. warm and stormy
   b. snowing
   c. sunny; not cloudy
   d. cloudy and rainy

3. Finish the following sentence to tell about an ice event in 2000.

   People in one city saw eight _____

   _____ hit a _____

   in the country of _____ .

4. What is one feature of ice bombs?
   a. They don't fall during storms. Instead, they usually fall during sunny weather.
   b. They are small, liké hail.
   c. They fall only in North America.
   d. all of the above

5. Read the following sentence from the story and answer the question.

   So far, scientists cannot tell us anything about the ice-bomb mystery.

   What other word for *mystery* could be used in this sentence?
   a. experiment
   b. event
   c. puzzle
   d. series

6. How did scientists know that the ice bomb in West Virginia was not spilled from an airplane?

   Scientists did not find any

   _____ in it.

7. Circle three adjectives that tell about ice bombs.

   huge   soft   sudden

   quiet   dark   mysterious

Can People Read Minds?

The phone rings. Even though you haven't talked to her all year, somehow you know it's your cousin . . . *before* you pick up the phone. Later, you are watching a TV show. Before the show gets to its surprise ending, you already know what is going to happen. The next day, you go to the mall with your brother. While you are still in the parking lot, you suddenly feel that he's going to find a blue shirt and buy it. And, he does!

Are these examples of *ESP*, or extrasensory perception? Some people think so. ESP is the ability to predict something that will happen. Some people who believe in ESP think that it is linked to reading another person's mind.

In the 1930s, a scientist named J. B. Rhine tested people to see if they had ESP. He used a set of five cards. Each card showed a simple picture: a plus sign, a square, a circle, a star, or three wavy lines. One person looked at a card. He thought hard about the picture on the card to "send" it. The other person tried to guess which picture was on the card by reading the sender's mind. Because there were five cards, each person had a chance of guessing one card right out of five. But, if someone got four out of five correct, Rhine thought that showed that the person had ESP.

Some people thought that Rhine's tests were bad. They said it might be too easy to cheat. Today, scientists have made harder tests. The "sender" looks at a picture on a TV screen. The "subject" is in a different room. The room is dim and quiet. The subject talks aloud about the picture that the sender is seeing. Later, the subject looks at the TV screen and tries to choose the pictures that were "sent." Many times, it doesn't work. Sometimes, the person tells about a picture in great detail. Is this ESP? Or, is it just luck? What do you think?

Next Page

Can People Read Minds?

Answer the questions below.

1. Which of the following is the BEST definition of ESP?
   a. reading cards with symbols on them
   b. knowing the ending to a TV show
   c. the ability to predict what will happen
   d. seeing a picture in your mind

2. Read the following sentence from the story and answer the question.

   Some people who believe in ESP think that it is linked to reading another person's mind.

   What is another word for *linked*?
   a. described
   b. connected
   c. sunk
   d. transferred

3. Which of the following is an opinion?
   a. ESP just has to be real because it is so interesting.
   b. Scientists are still testing people for ESP.
   c. J. B. Rhine was one of the first people who tested for ESP.
   d. Some people do not believe in ESP.

4. Why did some people think that J. B. Rhine's tests were bad? Write your answer in a complete sentence.

   _____

   _____

5.–7. Fill in the blanks to describe the sequence in J. B. Rhine's experiments.

5. J. B. Rhine's experiments used a total

   of _____ picture cards.

6. One person thought about the

   picture to " _____ " it.

7. The other person tried to guess the

   _____ .

8. Read the following sentence from the story and answer the question.

   The "subject" is in a different room.

   Which of the following is the definition of *subject* as it is used in the sentence?
   a. the servant of a king or leader
   b. a person whose responses or answers are studied
   c. the main topic of a report
   d. a field of study in school

Stars on Earth

Some people are looking up at a group of low hills in west Texas. Suddenly, they see glowing, red-orange lights. Are they the headlights of cars on the highway? Are they the lights of campfires? The people shout and point. The lights are moving! But, they aren't moving the way cars move. They go up in the air. They fall back to the earth. And then . . . they simply disappear!

Every night, people go to look at the famous Marfa lights. They are named for the town of Marfa, Texas. The lights can be seen east of the town when you look at the hills in the distance. There have been many theories about these strange lights over the years. One theory is that the lights are the headlights of cars driving down the road.

But, that could not be true. Settlers in the 1880s wrote about the lights. That was long before there were cars with headlights. At that time, pioneers thought the Marfa lights were the campfires of Apaches in the hills. When they would ride into the hills, they could not find evidence of campsites or fires. Later, the settlers learned that the Apaches, too, could see the lights. They said the lights were stars that had come down to Earth.

Some people say that the lights are moonlight shining on minerals in the hills. Others say they are made by gas from swamps. Some scientists have tried to prove that the lights really are light from planets or stars. They say this light is reflecting in a strange way on the hills. That doesn't help us understand why the lights can "dance." They move up and down, slow down, and speed up. These dancing "stars," the Marfa lights, stay a mystery.

Next Page

Stars on Earth

Answer the questions below.

1. Read the following sentence from the story and answer the question.

    And then . . . they simply disappear!

    Which of the following is an antonym for *disappear*?

    a. vanish
    b. leave
    c. appeal
    d. appear

2. From where did the Marfa lights get their name? Write your answer in a complete sentence.

    _____

    _____

    _____

3. Which of the following is NOT a feature of the Marfa lights?

    a. They are always blue-white.
    b. They move up and down.
    c. They can speed up and slow down.
    d. b. and c.

4.–8. Write T for true and F for false.

4. _____ Early settlers could not see the lights.

5. _____ The Apaches thought the lights were stars.

6. _____ People saw the lights before cars with headlights were invented.

7. _____ Early settlers thought the lights might be campfires.

8. _____ Some scientists think the lights are from stars or planets.

9. Choose the word that BEST completes the following sentence:

    The Marfa lights can be seen outside of Marfa toward the _____ .

    a. north
    b. west
    c. east
    d. south

10. Circle the phrase about the Marfa lights that is NOT a theory discussed in the story.

    reflected starlight

    lights from boats

    moonlight on minerals

    stars coming down to Earth

    swamp gas

The Green Children

It was a summer day in England in the 12th century. The villagers of Woolpit were at work in the fields. They heard crying. When they ran toward the sound, they found two young children. The children were talking in a strange language. Their clothes were odd. And, their skin was *green*!

When the villagers tried to feed the children, they only wanted to eat green beans. The little boy died. But, the girl lived and learned to speak English. After a while, her skin turned a normal color. She told people that she and her brother had come from a land where there was no sun. They had followed the sound of bells. The next thing they knew, they were in Woolpit.

People have added other notes to this story over the years. It is said that the children came from a country across a sea. One story was that the children said they had lived under the ground. People have wondered if the children were fairies or from outer space.

Maybe there is a simpler way to look at this story. In the 12th century, many people went to England from mainland Europe. Not all of these people were welcome. Some were killed in a battle in 1173. The children might have gotten lost after their parents died. There are many tunnels and mines near Woolpit. The children may have been lost in the tunnels and spent a long time underground. When they heard the church bells at Woolpit, they would have found their way out. Because they were starving, their skin could have taken on a green color. This was called "the green sickness." Today, we call it *anemia*. The children would have spoken the language of their parents, not English. However, because this happened so long ago, we may never know the truth for sure. Meanwhile, people still tell many different stories about the strange Green Children.

Next Page

The Green Children

Answer the questions below.

1. Which of the following theories about the Green Children's skin is NOT mentioned in the story?
   a. They were fairies.
   b. They were from outer space.
   c. They were the children of frogs.
   d. They had anemia.

2. Which of the following describes the Green Children?
   a. They would only eat beans.
   b. They wore strange clothing.
   c. They spoke in a strange language.
   d. all of the above

3. The Green Children were found near a village named _____ .

4. _____ of the children did not live.

5. The Green Children might have been lost in a _____ or mine.

6. When they were found, the Green Children did not speak _____ .

7. Which of the following sentences is an opinion?
   a. The Green Children were found by people working in a field.
   b. Only one of the children lived.
   c. People have added to the story over the years.
   d. It's too bad we will never know the whole truth about the Green Children.

8. Choose the phrase that BEST completes the following sentence:

   The 12th century was _____ .
   a. about 1200 A.D.
   b. about 1000 A.D.
   c. between 1200 A.D. and 1300 A.D.
   d. between 1100 A.D. and 1200 A.D.

9. What do you think happened to the Green Children? Why do you think so? Write your answer in complete sentences.

   _____

   _____

   _____

   _____

   _____

STOP

Footprints in the Snow

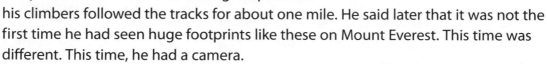

In 1951, Eric Shipton was climbing Mount Everest, the highest mountain in the world. He and his team were exploring when they saw a scary sight. There were giant footprints in the snow! It looked like huge bare feet had made them. Each footprint was about 13 inches long. Shipton and his climbers followed the tracks for about one mile. He said later that it was not the first time he had seen huge footprints like these on Mount Everest. This time was different. This time, he had a camera.

Eric Shipton was a famous explorer. His pictures of the giant footprints created excitement all over the world. And, there was more to the story. A man named Sen Tensing was one of Shipton's guides. Tensing said that he and others had once seen the creature that had made the prints. He said that it was a *yeti*, a wild man. This barefoot creature had reddish-brown fur on half of his body. The yeti was over five feet tall. Shipton had someone question Tensing about the event. Shipton said that he believed Tensing. The explorer also said that he was sure the footprints were not made by a bear or a mountain ape.

Others are not so sure. Some think that the huge footprints were made by a bear that lives in the mountains and often walks on two legs. But, Shipton and his men followed the tracks for one mile. Would a bear have walked that far on two legs when it could run on four? Others say that Tensing saw a mountain ape. But, mountain apes have five toes, and these footprints had only four. Some scientists think that the footprints were made by a smaller animal. Then, the sun melted them so that they looked bigger. Shipton said that the footprints were fresh. Could the sun have had time to melt them? Or, did the explorers really find the footprints of a strange, wild man of the mountain?

Conversions

13 inches = 33.02 centimeters
1 mile = 1.61 kilometers
5 feet = 1.52 meters

Next Page

Name _____ Date _____

Footprints in the Snow

Answer the questions below.

1. What is a *yeti*? Write your answer in a complete sentence.

   _____

   _____

2. Tensing said the yeti he saw had all of the following features EXCEPT—
   a. reddish-brown fur.
   b. bare feet.
   c. fur all over his body.
   d. large feet.

3.–7. Write T for true and F for false.

3. _____ Eric Shipton was an explorer in the 1950s.

4. _____ Shipton saw strange tracks in the snow on Mount Fuji.

5. _____ Sen Tensing was Shipton's personal chef.

6. _____ Some scientists think the footprints melted in the sun.

7. _____ Mountain apes have four toes on each foot.

8. Choose the phrase that BEST completes the following sentence:

   Mount Everest is _____.
   a. in North America
   b. the tallest mountain on Earth
   c. a mountain range in Asia
   d. none of the above

9. The explorers followed the strange tracks in the snow for—
   a. one yard.
   b. one kilometer.
   c. 1,000 yards.
   d. one mile.

10. Eric Shipton probably did not believe that the tracks were made by a bear because—
    a. bears have three toes on each foot.
    b. bears do not walk that far on two legs.
    c. bears do not have reddish-brown fur.
    d. bears do not have large feet.

Conversions

1 yard = 0.91 meters
1 kilometer = 0.62 mile
1,000 yards = 914.4 meters
1 mile = 1.61 kilometers

Honest Abe's Return

Do you believe in ghosts? If you lived at the White House or ever spent the night there, you might. That's because this famous American house seems to be haunted. And, its most famous ghost is President Abraham Lincoln!

Workers in the White House say they have seen Lincoln's ghost many times. One man said he saw Lincoln sitting outside of a room. The room had once been his office. Workers say they have also seen doors close by themselves. Lights turn on by themselves near this room. The workers think that the ghost of President Lincoln could be doing these things.

Other people claim to have seen Lincoln's ghost, too. Queen Wilhelmina of the Netherlands once stayed in the White House. She heard a knock at the door. When she opened it, Lincoln's ghost was standing there. The queen fainted.

Winston Churchill, the famous British leader, also said he saw the ghost. The room that was Lincoln's office was later made into a bedroom. Churchill stayed there. He walked into the bedroom. There was Lincoln, standing next to the fireplace. In fact, the "Lincoln Bedroom" is the place where the ghost is seen most often. One First Lady, Grace Coolidge, said that she saw Lincoln looking sadly out the window there. President Reagan's dog would not even go into the Lincoln Bedroom. The dog just stood at the door and barked!

Even the official White House Web site shares stories about Lincoln's ghost. On the site, you can listen to people tell stories about the ghost. These people all say that they have seen the ghost of President Lincoln . . . more than 100 years after his death.

Next Page

Honest Abe's Return

Answer the questions below.

1. Read the following sentence from the story and answer the question.

   One First Lady, Grace Coolidge, said that she saw Lincoln looking sadly out the window there.

   What is a *First Lady*?
   a. a female President
   b. the first woman who lived in the White House
   c. the wife of a President
   d. the daughter of a President

2. The ghost of President Lincoln is said to haunt—
   a. the White House.
   b. his former office.
   c. the Lincoln Bedroom.
   d. all of the above

3. Which of the following is NOT a fact?
   a. Workers in the White House say that they have seen Lincoln's ghost.
   b. The Queen of the Netherlands fainted when she thought she saw the ghost.
   c. It must be very scary to see a ghost in the Lincoln Bedroom.
   d. The official White House Web site has stories about the ghost.

4. Which of the following is NOT in the story?
   a. how Abraham Lincoln died
   b. where Winston Churchill said he saw the ghost
   c. how President Reagan's dog acted outside the Lincoln Bedroom
   d. which First Lady thought she saw the ghost

5. Which of the following BEST states the main idea of the story?
   a. Many people have told stories about seeing the ghost of Lincoln in the White House.
   b. The Queen of the Netherlands fainted when she thought she saw the ghost.
   c. Dogs do not like ghosts.
   d. Lincoln ghost stories may or may not be true.

6. Circle *do* or *do not*. Then, finish the sentence.

   I (**do** , **do not**) believe in ghosts

   because _____

   _____

   _____

   _____ .

Lights from the Deep

People talk a lot about *UFOs*, or unidentified flying objects. There are many stories about these strange, flying objects. But, the sky is not the only place where people think they see UFOs. Many people have claimed to see objects moving in the sea, too. These lights are called USOs. The "S" stands for "submarine." The word *submarine* means "under the sea."

In 1909, a ship called the *Bintang* filed a report. The crew said they saw strange lights in the sea. The lights looked like a giant wheel. It was turning clockwise and moving quickly. It passed the ship. Then, it slowed down . . . and vanished!

That was not the first time that a USO was reported. In 1881, two sons of the Prince of Wales were on a ship in the Pacific Ocean. They said they saw a glowing ship pass under their boat. Twelve crew members also saw the strange sight.

There are more recent reports, too. In 1976, two sailors saw circles of light go under their ship. They thought they saw an even brighter light shining up from deep in the sea. And, in 1980, the crew of a boat near Brazil reported a long, gray object moving very quickly under the water. A big light followed it above the water. The object and the light moved swiftly past the boat.

Reports about the lights differ. One ship saw a big wheel moving under the water. Other ships have seen smaller lights that seem to be traveling in a group. But, what could the lights be? Some people wonder if the ships could be from an underwater city. If some scientists think there might be people living on other planets, then why not in the deep parts of our own oceans, too?

Next Page

Lights from the Deep

Answer the questions below.

1. Read the following sentence from the story and answer the question.

   In 1909, a ship called the *Bintang* filed a report.

   Which of the following is the definition of *filed* as it is used in the sentence?

   a. to enter something as an official story
   b. to smooth rough edges
   c. to put something in alphabetical order
   d. to use a tool made of steel with ridges

2. Which of the following sentences about USOs is true?

   a. Only one ship ever reported seeing lights under the water.
   b. Two sons of the Queen of England saw the lights.
   c. One ship saw a giant wheel, turning clockwise.
   d. Other ships have seen spacemen on the lighted boats.

3. What do the "S" in USO and the "F" in UFO mean?

   a. "silly" and "flighty"
   b. "submarine" and "flying"
   c. "scary" and "fearful"
   d. "strong" and "fighting"

4. The story mentions all of the following USOs EXCEPT—

   a. a giant wheel of lights.
   b. a gray object moving very fast.
   c. lights shaped like a whale.
   d. a. and b.

5. *Glowing* means—

   a. shining with light from the inside.
   b. frowning.
   c. smoothing over.
   d. putting together with glue.

6. *Differ* means—

   a. the distance between objects.
   b. not agreeing.
   c. not truthful.
   d. fast or swift.

7. Fill in the sentence with your own theory about USOs.

   I think the lights could be _____

   _____

   because _____

   _____

   _____ .

The Ink Monkey

In China, there are stories about tiny monkeys that lived long ago. Each little creature weighed only seven ounces. The stories say that these monkeys were very smart. They were so smart that people trained them to do chores. Children in China tell stories about "the ink monkey." It was the pet of a famous thinker named Zhu Xi during the 12th century. It sat on his desk. The monkey handed him pens when he was writing. It helped him make ink.

For hundreds of years, people thought that the story about the ink monkey was just a story. Think about a monkey so small that it could sleep in a paintbrush pot! Picture an animal so smart that it could learn to make ink and help someone write. It had to be fiction!

But, in 2000, an American scientist found something in China. He found the bones of an ancient monkey. This monkey had been as small as a mouse. It was so tiny that the bones in its feet were as small as grains of rice. The scientist, Dan Gebo, says that this monkey may be a *missing link*. That is an animal that can tell us more about how humans evolved. Gebo calls his find "the dawn monkey."

Could the dawn monkey be linked to the ink monkey? The dawn monkey is much smaller than we thought monkeys could be. We now know that millions of years ago, there really was a mouse-sized monkey living in China. Could this be the ancestor of Zhu Xi's pet?

Soon after Dr. Gebo's important discovery came another surprise. The Chinese said that they had found a living ink monkey. They said it was found in the forest where Zhu Xi once lived. But, they have not yet let other scientists know more.

Conversion

7 ounces = 198.45 grams

The Ink Monkey

Answer the questions below.

1.–5. Match each word to its antonym.

1. _____ tiny   a. boring

2. _____ famous   b. dead

3. _____ interesting   c. huge

4. _____ living   d. new

5. _____ ancient   e. unknown

6. The "ink monkey" was the pet of—
   a. Dan Gebo.
   b. Li Xi.
   c. the dawn monkey.
   d. Zhu Xi.

7. Read the following sentences from the story and answer the question.

   Picture an animal so smart that it could learn to make ink and help someone write. It had to be fiction!

   What is another way of saying *It had to be fiction*?
   a. It had to be a discovery.
   b. It had to be just a story.
   c. It had to be true.
   d. It had to be factual.

8. An animal that helps us understand how humans evolved is called a

   _____ .

9. The "dawn monkey's" bones were

   discovered by _____ .

10. The "dawn monkey" might be the

    ink monkey's _____ .

11. The "dawn monkey" was the size of—
    a. a grain of rice.
    b. a squirrel.
    c. a mouse.
    d. a bird.

12. Do you believe there was an ink monkey, or do you think the story is fiction? Why do you think so? Write your answer in complete sentences.

    _____

    _____

    _____

    _____

Friend or Foe?

When the cat, Huan, cornered the baby mouse in a closet, it was easy to predict the end of the story—a meal for Huan and a very short life for the mouse. But, sometimes in the animal world, stories do not turn out as you think they might. Huan, who had hunted and eaten mice her whole life, did not kill this baby mouse. Instead, she became friends with it.

Huan's owner started calling the baby mouse Jerry. Jerry and Huan spent every day together. They played together. They slept in the same bed. They drank milk from the same bowl. Huan kept other cats away from Jerry. Jerry cleaned Huan's paws for her.

What's going on here? How could two animals who are supposed to be enemies become friends?

This strange twist in the animal world happens from time to time. No scientist can explain how this sudden trust between animals happens. Once, the owners of a wildlife park in Arizona planned an experiment. They put four mountain lions, four gray wolves, and four black bears together in one part of the park. These animals are natural enemies. Would they hurt each other? The owners thought that they would not. They were right. A female wolf took the lead. She went to the group of mountain lions and lay down on the ground. She let the lions sniff her. Soon, these enemies were playing together. Then, the wolf made friends with the bears, too. Why did it turn out so well? No one knows why it happens.

Sometimes, different animals take care of *orphans*—animals or people who have lost their parents. This can even happen when the orphan isn't the same kind of animal as the new mother! For example, in Africa, a baby hippo lost its mother in a big storm. When it was taken to a wildlife park, the little hippo was adopted by a giant tortoise! The tortoise decided to take care of the hippo as if it were her own baby.

Next Page ➡

Friend or Foe?

Answer the questions below.

1. _____ was a cat that made friends with a mouse.

2. One of the enemies of the gray wolf is _____ .

3. A mother _____ adopted a baby hippo.

4. The owners of a wildlife park in _____ did an experiment to see if animal enemies could become friends.

5. Read the following sentence from the story and answer the question.

   When the cat, Huan, cornered the baby mouse in a closet, it was easy to predict the end of the story—a meal for Huan and a very short life for the mouse.

   Which of the following words would BEST replace *cornered* in this sentence?
   a. angled
   b. chased
   c. caged
   d. trapped

6. The story mentions all of the following animals EXCEPT—
   a. a mountain lion
   b. a mouse
   c. an owl
   d. a black bear

7. Look at the title of this story. Which of the following is an antonym for *foe*?
   a. enemy
   b. advisor
   c. villain
   d. friend

8. The author says that scientists cannot explain how a sudden trust happens between animals. Write three of your own theories about how or why it may happen.

   a. _____

   _____

   b. _____

   _____

   c. _____

   _____

Taking Flight

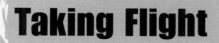

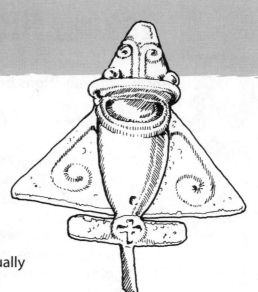

Everyone knows that the Wright brothers made the first working airplane. Or did they? Scientists have made some strange finds. They seem to show that people thought about building airplanes long ago. Did they actually make these flying machines?

A model of a flying object was found in a tomb in Egypt. Explorers found it and put it in a box marked "wooden bird model." That was in 1898, before a working airplane was invented. Years later, another scientist opened the box. By then, a working airplane had been invented. The scientist had seen an airplane, so he knew the model was not a bird! The model looks just like a glider plane. It even has curved wings, like the ones on the Concorde jet. This model was made about 200 B.C. In Egypt, builders often made small models of things they planned to build. Did they build this airplane?

Another strange thing was found in Central America. It is a small, gold model with wings. The people of Colombia made many little gold animals. These gold trinkets are found in tombs. But, this model does not look like a bird. It does not look like a bug. It looks like a strange little airplane. Was it meant to be a flying machine?

Then, there are ancient stories from India. These texts were written more than 2,000 years ago. The authors were called "The Nine Unknown Men." In these writings, it says that the ancient Indians knew how to fly. They had airplanes shaped like circles. These circles had domed ceilings. They had *portholes*, or windows, all around them. They sound like flying saucers! The stories tell how these machines flew "with the speed of the wind." Is this proof that ancient people built airplanes?

Taking Flight

Answer the questions below.

1. Which of the following statements is an opinion?
   a. A wooden model that looks like an airplane was found in Egypt.
   b. If there were ancient flying machines, that would be the most exciting discovery ever.
   c. The Colombians made small, gold objects that have been found in tombs.
   d. The Wright brothers made the first airplane that flew well.

2. Which of the following sentences is NOT true?
   a. The "Nine Unknown Men" wrote in about 1000 A.D.
   b. Explorers found a wooden model in a tomb.
   c. The "wooden bird model" was made about 200 B.C.
   d. The Egyptian model and the Indian writings were both done over 2,000 years ago.

3. Read the following sentences from the story and answer the question.

   The people of Colombia made many little gold animals. These gold trinkets are found in tombs.

   What is a word that could replace *trinkets*?
   a. coffins
   b. furniture
   c. clothes
   d. ornaments

4. Why did the explorers who found the wooden model think it looked like a bird and not an airplane?
   a. In 1898, airplanes looked different.
   b. The explorers didn't look at it carefully.
   c. In 1898, few people knew what an airplane was.
   d. The explorers had bad eyesight.

5. Which of the following is NOT talked about in the story?
   a. a small, gold airplane from Colombia
   b. a model found in a tomb in Egypt
   c. drawings of airplanes by Leonardo da Vinci
   d. ancient Indian stories about flying machines

6. Do you think ancient people built flying machines? Why or why not? Write your answer in complete sentences.

   _____

   _____

   _____

   _____

STOP

It's Raining Cats and . . . Frogs?

Have you had any strange weather in your town this week? Even if you have, it probably won't top September 7, 1953. That's the day it rained frogs and toads in the town of Leicester, Massachusetts! The streets were covered with leaping frogs. Children filled buckets with them. A newspaper said the frogs and toads hopped out of a pond that had overflowed. But, people said they saw the frogs and toads fall from the sky. They found them on roofs of houses.

This "frogfall" was probably less scary than what happened in Memphis, Tennessee, in 1877. There, it rained black snakes! The snakes ranged from one foot long to 1.5 feet long. There were thousands of them. People thought the snakes might have been swept into a huge windstorm. When the storm ended, the snakes fell from the sky. But, if that were true, why didn't twigs, stones, and other things fall along with the snakes? It was strange that only snakes would have been swept from the ground and nothing else.

It's easy to see how a rain of animals from the sea or a lake could happen during a big storm. Sometimes, water from a pond is sucked up by a huge wind. Then, it is rained down somewhere else. Maybe that's what happened in Tiller's Ferry, South Carolina, in 1901. It rained fish there! Trout and catfish fell in a heavy rain from the sky. After the storm, fish were found swimming in puddles in the cotton fields.

There are many reports of strange things falling from the sky. Other places have had "rains" of rocks, golf balls, ducks, and even candy! Keep your eyes open for the next interesting storm. It might be in *your* town.

Conversions
1 foot = 30.48 centimeters
1.5 feet = 45.72 centimeters

It's Raining Cats and . . . Frogs?

Answer the questions below.

1. Read the following sentences from the story and answer the question.

   Keep your eyes open for the next interesting storm. It might be in *your* town.

   Which phrase could BEST be used to replace *Keep your eyes open*?

   a. stay awake
   b. wake up
   c. stay alert
   d. open your eyes wide

2. The story mentions all of the following strange weather events EXCEPT—

   a. raining snakes.
   b. raining candy.
   c. raining baseballs.
   d. raining toads.

3. Which of the following is the definition of *overflowed* as it is used in the story?

   a. left its borders or boundaries
   b. coming out of a spring
   c. overly concerned
   d. oversight

4. The title of this story is based on the phrase, "It's raining cats and dogs." What kind of expression is this?

   a. a metaphor
   b. a simile
   c. an idiom
   d. onomatopoeia

5.–8. Write T for true and F for false.

5. _____ Snakes rained down on the town of Leicester in Massachusetts.

6. _____ Some of the strange weather events have happened after windstorms.

7. _____ Catfish and dogfish rained down on Tiller's Ferry, South Carolina.

8. _____ The story tells about places that have had "rainfalls" of rocks, ducks, and chalk.

9. What was the author's purpose in writing this article?

   a. to inform
   b. to entertain
   c. to persuade
   d. a. and b.

The Ghost of a King?

Hampton Court was one home of King Henry VIII of England. Today, hundreds of visitors flock to the beautiful palace. While they are there, they hear stories about ghosts at the royal home. But, everyone was surprised when one of those ghosts appeared on TV!

In October 2003, guards at the palace had trouble with one of the fire exits. The doors kept opening. The guards watched the security camera films. Once, the camera caught the doors flying open by themselves. Nobody could say how it had happened.

On October 7, a visitor said she thought she had seen a ghost. Then, the guards were told that the fire doors had opened again. They checked their film. What they saw scared them. A man in a long cloak, with a spooky white face, opened the door. Then, he closed it. The clothes he wore were from the time of King Henry VIII!

The guards who worked at the palace checked all of the staff. Some of them wear costumes. No one had a costume like the one on the film. Even after they had questioned everybody, they could not find a staff member who had opened the door. Also, as one of the guards said, "The face just didn't look human."

Somehow, the press got copies of the film. Everyone had a theory about this strange event. Some people looked at still shots from the film. They said the still pictures made the person look less like a ghost. Some thought it might have been a visitor in a long coat who closed the doors. And, some people said that a ghost from the 1500s would not know how to close a modern fire door!

Others say that the film was not staged, but real. Some even wonder if this is Henry VIII himself. Could the restless king still be wandering the halls of his old palace home?

Name _____ Date _____

The Ghost of a King?

Answer the questions below.

1. What is a *palace*?
   a. a castle
   b. the place where a king or queen lives
   c. a royal home
   d. all of the above

2. Read the following sentences from the story and answer the question.

   The guards who worked at the palace checked all of the staff. Some of them wear costumes. No one had a costume like the one on the film.

   Why do you think that the author included this information?
   a. to show that the guards were smart
   b. so that the reader would know that the guards couldn't find a person who had worn the clothing in the film
   c. so that the reader would know the person was a staff member
   d. to show that the security at Hampton Court is very good

3. What is a *security camera*?
   a. a camera used by tourists to take pictures of palaces
   b. a camera used to watch different parts of a building
   c. a camera used to take pictures of famous people, like kings
   d. a camera used by guards to take pictures of criminals after they are caught

4. Which sentence BEST summarizes the main idea of the story?
   a. Hampton Court is the former home of King Henry VIII.
   b. At Hampton Court, a ghost opens fire exit doors.
   c. Security films from Hampton Court show someone opening a door, and some say it is a ghost.
   d. Henry VIII opens fire exit doors at Hampton Court, and no one knows why he does it.

5. Another term for worker is a

   "member of the _____."

6. How do you write "VIII" as a word?

   _____

7. Do you think that the person on the film was a ghost? Why or why not? Write your answer in complete sentences.

   _____

   _____

   _____

   _____

STOP

Crop Circles

Are they messages to pilots from other worlds? Are they works of art? Are they proof of UFO landings? People have talked about crop circles for hundreds of years. People can't agree about how they show up . . . or why.

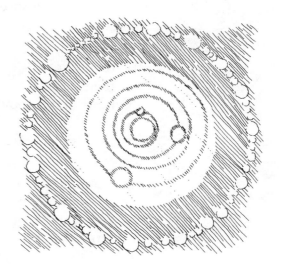

Crop circles are huge patterns found in fields. Many are large circles. Sometimes, there are smaller circles around them. But, they can be any pattern. The crop, such as wheat or corn, has been crushed or laid out flat. That's what makes the pattern in the field.

The first crop circles that we know about were found in England during the 17th century. Hundreds of crop circles have been found since then. Today, the strange patterns show up in fields all around the world. Are they made by people or by something else?

A group called the Circle Makers says that they have made many of the crop circles that are reported. These people think of themselves as artists. They use boards to sweep over the crops. They use ropes or strings to pull the boards. Sometimes, they use computers to help them plan their crop circles.

Other people point to crop circles that were not made by the Circle Makers or by other groups. Could these crop circles have been made by nature? Some scientists think that strange weather patterns make the circles and other patterns. Still other people think that the crop circles show where UFOs have landed.

And, here is something else that is strange—some members of the Circle Makers say that when they work in the fields, things happen that they can't explain. They see lights in the sky. One artist even saw a strange silver object flying over the field. Could it be that these human-made crop circles are watched from outer space?

Next Page

Crop Circles

Answer the questions below.

1. The author's purpose in writing this article is—
   a. to persuade.
   b. to inform.
   c. to inspire.
   d. none of the above

2. Which of the following is the BEST description of a crop circle?
   a. a pattern that is made with boards and ropes
   b. something that is used to attract UFOs
   c. strange patterns that are made in fields of wheat or corn
   d. tricks that are played by people

3. Read the following sentence from the story and answer the question.

   The first crop circles that we know about were found in England during the 17th century.

   What do the words *that we know about* tell the reader?
   a. There were many crop circles found after the 17th century.
   b. We don't know about all of the crop circles found in the 17th century.
   c. There might have been other crop circles before the 17th century, but no writings about them exist.
   d. There were definitely other crop circles before the 17th century.

4. Read the following sentence from the story and answer the question.

   Are they messages to pilots from other worlds?

   Which of the following words could replace *messages*?
   a. reports
   b. trash
   c. distances
   d. poems

5. The _____

   are a group who say they have

   created many of the crop circles.

6. Write three ideas from the story about how crop circles might be made. Use complete sentences.

   a. _____

   _____

   b. _____

   _____

   c. _____

   _____

Flores Man Floors Scientists

The scientists could not believe their eyes. They had found something strange. It was a skeleton of a being that looks like a human who was only three feet tall! Around the skeleton were the bones and teeth of other small creatures. The scientists also found tiny tools that these beings had made.

These scientists were on the island of Flores. That's where they made this important find. Flores is an island in the Pacific Ocean. Long ago, it was a strange place. Giant lizards and tiny elephants lived in the jungle there. "Flores Man" lived on the island, too. He hunted these animals for food. All living things on the island may have been killed about 12,000 years ago. That's when a volcano blew up. But, there are stories that Flores Man survived. It is said that these tiny people were seen by Dutch explorers in the 1500s.

In the world of science, 12,000 years is not very long. One thing that is surprising is that we didn't know about Flores Man before the discovery in 2003. But, the island of Flores has not been explored very much. The skeleton and bones were in wet earth. Scientists say that the bones were like "mashed potatoes." Maybe other bones were destroyed by mistake.

Many people agree that the discovery of Flores Man is big news. Some scientists say that this missing race shows us that man did not evolve the way that we once thought. Other scientists do not agree.

Make a prediction.

What do you think the author will write about next? Circle your answer.

Flores Man's home   theories about Flores Man   what made Flores Man extinct

Conversion

3 feet = 0.91 meter

Next Page

Answer the following questions based on what you read on page 31. Then, finish reading the story at the bottom of the page.

1. What is an antonym for *surprising*?

   a. amazing
   b. strange
   c. expected
   d. difficult

2. Where is Flores?

   a. in the Indian Ocean
   b. in the Atlantic Ocean
   c. in the North Sea
   d. in the Pacific Ocean

3. What is "Flores Man"? Write your answer in a complete sentence.

   _____

   _____

   _____

4. Circle three words or phrases that BEST describe Flores Man.

   tiny   good swimmer   mysterious

   elephant   seen by tourists   hunter

   wiped out by sickness

Some scientists think that Flores Man might not have been human at all. They say the small body size and the large features of the face do not look enough like an early human. Some scientists also point to the small brain size of Flores Man. It was only one-third the size of our brains today. Others are sure that Flores Man is from the same family as today's humans. Many scientists do not agree about where Flores Man fits in the chain of the human family.

Things may become clearer after more exploration. Scientists plan to go back to the island of Flores and the other islands around it. They hope to find more bones and other objects. These discoveries will help them learn more about Flores Man.

Next Page ➤

Flores Man Floors Scientists

Answer the questions below.

5. Read the following sentence from the story and answer the question.

   The scientists could not believe their eyes.

   What kind of phrase is *could not believe their eyes*?

   a. a metaphor
   b. a simile
   c. a figure of speech
   d. all of the above

6. Choose the BEST summary of the argument about Flores Man.

   a. Some scientists think that Flores Man was from the human species and others do not.
   b. Some scientists think that Flores Man was a tiny human and others think he was larger.
   c. Some scientists think that Flores Man was seen in the 1500s.
   d. Some scientists think that Flores Man was not found earlier because other bones might have been overlooked.

7. Which of the following is an opinion?

   a. The island of Flores has not been explored very much.
   b. Flores Man made tiny tools that were found on the dig.
   c. Flores Man is the most exciting scientific find in many years.
   d. Flores Man had about one-third the brain size of today's humans.

8. The bones found in the wet earth were compared to which food?

   a. ice cream
   b. mashed carrots
   c. bread
   d. mashed potatoes

9. Read the following sentence from the story and answer the question.

   They say the small body size and the large features of the face do not look enough like an early human.

   Which of the following is an example of a *feature of the face*?

   a. hair
   b. neck
   c. nose
   d. fingers

10. Which of the following is NOT true?

   a. Scientists do not agree that Flores Man was from the human family.
   b. Flores Man seems to have been a hunter.
   c. Scientists found jewelry that Flores Man made.
   d. Scientists plan to continue exploring the island of Flores for bones and other finds.

The Missing Mine

The year was 1846. A family from Mexico was living in Arizona. They were there to mine in the mountains. When they dug in their mine, they found gold. Not just a few gold nuggets, but huge quantities of gold! The family sent millions of dollars worth of gold from the mine to their home in Mexico. Then, trouble started. The Apaches were angry that the miners were on their land. By 1848, the owner of the mine knew that he had to leave. He closed the mine. He hid the entrance. He and his workers loaded up their mules with their last bags of gold. But, before they could leave, the Apaches killed them. The gold from the bags was worthless to the Apaches. It was scattered across the plains.

How did other people learn about the vast gold mine? People searched and found the gold that the workers had carried. Even 75 years later, people were still finding gold from that last 1848 load. In 1914, one man found $18,000 worth of gold in one day!

Many people looked for the mine itself. They could not find it. The mine remained hidden. But, that is not the end of the story. In the 1870s, a German man named Jacob Walz came to Arizona. He had visited with members of the mine owner's family in Mexico. They told him stories about the entrance to the mine. He was sure that he could find it. And, when he did, he would be rich!

Make a prediction.

What do you think the author will write about next?

_____

Answer the following questions based on what you read on page 34. Then, finish reading the story at the bottom of the page.

1. Read the following sentence from the story and answer the question.

   The gold from the bags was worthless to the Apaches.

   Which of the following is the BEST meaning of *worthless*?

   a. meaningless
   b. without taste
   c. without value
   d. hopeless

2. Where was Jacob Walz from?

   a. Holland
   b. Mexico
   c. Germany
   d. Canada

3. What happened to the entrance to the mine in 1848?

   a. It was hidden by the Apaches.
   b. It was hidden by Jacob Walz.
   c. It was hidden by the head of the Mexican family who discovered it.
   d. It was hidden by a worker who wanted to steal the gold.

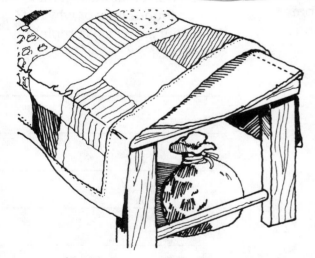

Jacob Walz was called "the Dutchman" in Phoenix, Arizona, a town near the mountains. For a while, he was a worker in other people's mines. He and a friend worked together in the same mountains where the lost gold mine was hidden. They came into town from time to time. When they did, they paid for things with gold nuggets. The gold they had was very pure. It wasn't like the gold mixtures, or gold *ore*, that other people found in the mountains. Was it coming from the lost mine?

After Jacob's friend died, he kept mining by himself. People tried to follow Jacob into the mountains, but he always disappeared and could not be tracked. For 20 years, he went out to the mountain and came back with sacks of gold. He became friends with a woman named Julia Thomas. She owned a bakery. One winter, he promised Julia he would take her out to the mountain and show her the place where he got his gold. But, he died not long after that. There was a huge sack of gold under his bed. Hundreds of people since then have tried to find the "Lost Dutchman Mine." They never have.

Next Page →

Name _____ Date _____

The Missing Mine

Answer the questions below.

4.–7. Write T for true and F for false.

4. _____ Jacob Walz was Dutch.

5. _____ Jacob Walz's nickname was "the Dutchman."

6. _____ Nobody knows exactly where Jacob got his gold.

7. _____ Julia Thomas owned a grocery store.

8. Read the following sentences from the story and answer the question.

    They came into town from time to time. When they did, they paid for things with gold nuggets.

    What is a *gold nugget*?
    a. gold dust
    b. a small piece of gold
    c. a gold charm
    d. a gold coin

9. Which of the following statements is a fact from the story?
    a. The Lost Dutchman Mine is near Phoenix, Arizona.
    b. Jacob Walz must have been very rich when he died.
    c. The mine is probably the most valuable mine on Earth.
    d. It is likely that the mystery of the lost mine will never be solved.

10. After 1848, how did people find out about the hidden riches in the mine?
    a. They found the entrance to the mine and saw the gold.
    b. They heard stories from the Apaches about the lost mine.
    c. They found the gold from the last load that the Apaches had left behind.
    d. They met with members of the family in Mexico who took them to the mine.

11. Do you think that the lost mine will ever be found? Why or why not? Write your answer in complete sentences.

    _____
    _____
    _____
    _____
    _____
    _____
    _____

The Pit of the Pirates

In 1795, a young boy named Daniel McGinnis rowed to Oak Island, an island off the coast of Canada. No one lived there. But, Daniel had heard stories about pirates who may have been on the island. He wanted to explore.

Daniel found a strange, sunken area near a tree. Later, he said that when he looked up in the tree, he saw a pulley. He rowed back home. A few days later, he brought two friends and shovels to the island. The boys started to dig. First, they found a layer of stones. Then, they found a layer of logs. Would there be treasure underneath them? Instead, there was just more dirt. But, they could tell that someone had dug up the dirt in the past. The boys dug 30 feet deep. They found two more layers of logs. Then, they gave up.

That was just the start of the adventure of the "Oak Island Money Pit." The boys returned to the island eight years later. This time, they brought help. They dug a hole 90 feet deep. There, they found a strange stone. It was carved with squares, triangles, and other symbols. Was it a code? Did it tell about treasure?

The next day, the diggers came back. The pit was filled with water! Later, people would say that the Oak Island Money Pit was booby-trapped. Whoever dug the pit had built a system of drains. Water came in from a nearby beach. Over and over, people tried to dig in the pit. Each time, it filled with water.

Make a prediction.

What do you think the author will write about next? Circle your answer.

Oak Island before 1795   other finds in the pit   pirates who lived on the island

Conversions

30 feet = 9.14 meters
90 feet = 27.43 meters

Name _____ Date _____

Answer the following questions based on what you read on page 37. Then, finish reading the story at the bottom of the page.

1. A boy named _____ was the first person to find the money pit.

2. The first time the three boys dug in the pit, they reached a depth of _____ .

3. Oak Island is off the coast of _____ .

4. Daniel thought that the pit held something buried by _____ .

5. At 90 feet deep, the diggers found—
   a. a gold chain.
   b. a strange map.
   c. a rock carved with symbols.
   d. b. and c.

6. Workers could not dig deeper because—
   a. the pit filled with water.
   b. the pit caved in.
   c. they were too tired.
   d. all of the above

People have been digging and trying to explore the Oak Island Money Pit for more than 200 years. Some people say that the rock with the code says that there is a huge treasure buried there. But, no one can find it.

One man found another rock on the island. It, too, had a code on it. But, the code couldn't be broken. The only other things found in the pit so far have been a piece of gold chain, a tiny piece of paper with writing on it, and a pair of 300-year-old scissors. Millions of dollars have been spent digging in the pit. Six people have died trying to find the treasure. Is there even a treasure there? A few people think that the money pit is just a natural tunnel. It is flooded by the sea. Many other people think that pirate gold will be found there someday.

© Carson-Dellosa

The Pit of the Pirates

Answer the questions below.

7. Read the following sentence from the story and answer the question.

   Later, people would say that the Oak Island Money Pit was booby-trapped.

   What is a *booby trap*?
   a. a trap to catch animals
   b. a hidden trap set to go off if something gets too close
   c. a practical joke
   d. a trap used in mining

8. Which of the following sentences BEST summarizes the story?
   a. Since 1795, many people have tried to find treasure in the Oak Island Money Pit, but no one has succeeded.
   b. Some people say the Oak Island Money Pit is a natural tunnel.
   c. The coded rock found in the Oak Island Money Pit says that there is treasure buried at the bottom of the pit.
   d. The Oak Island Money Pit fills with water when people try to dig in it.

9. Which of these was NOT found in the money pit?
   a. a pair of scissors
   b. a piece of gold chain
   c. a carved rock
   d. a Spanish coin

10. Look at the chain of events below and answer the question.

Daniel finds a pulley in a tree.
Daniel and his friends return eight years later.
Daniel and his friends find a carved rock that may have a code on it.
The money pit may be a booby trap and fills with water.

Which step is missing?
   a. Six people died trying to reach the treasure.
   b. Daniel and his two friends dig down to 30 feet.
   c. A pair of 300-year-old scissors is found.
   d. Pirate treasure is found.

11. Do you think there is treasure on Oak Island? Why or why not? Write your answer in complete sentences.

   _____

   _____

   _____

   _____

STOP

Monster in the Loch

The Scottish word for "lake" is *loch*. Loch Ness in Scotland is one of the deepest bodies of water in the world. But, that is not why it is famous. It is famous for something else—a monster. People say that a giant, swimming monster lives in the lake. It is said to be dark in color. It has a small head and a long neck. It swims like a seal but is as big as a bus. Some people say it looks like a dinosaur.

Is this monster real? We know that the stories about it are very old. When Roman soldiers first came to Scotland, they heard about strange animals in the lake. They even found a carving of a huge, swimming creature. Written records of the Loch Ness Monster go back to 565 A.D. But, reports soared in the 1930s. That was when a road was built around one side of the lake. For the first time, people could get close to the north side of Loch Ness. People started to see a huge, dark, diving animal. They saw the waves it made in the lake. There was great excitement. A circus owner offered thousands of dollars to anyone who could catch the creature for him!

People who live near Loch Ness say that they see the black, swimming animal all of the time. A few years ago, a man training for the Coast Guard found what might be a big, underwater cave. Could this be the place where the Loch Ness Monster and its family live? Other people point to tricks that were played. They say these tricks prove that the monster cannot be real.

Make a prediction.

What do you think the story will describe next?

_____

© Carson-Dellosa

Name_____ Date_____

Answer the following questions based on what you read on page 40. Then, finish reading the story at the bottom of the page.

1. What is a *loch*?
   a. a monster
   b. a sea
   c. a stream
   d. a lake

2. Read the following sentence from the story and answer the question.

   It swims like a seal but is as big as a bus.

   What kind of phrase is *as big as a bus*?
   a. a metaphor
   b. personification
   c. an idiom
   d. a simile

3. Write three words or phrases that describe the Loch Ness Monster.

   a. _____

   _____

   b. _____

   _____

   c. _____

   _____

Most people who say they have seen the Loch Ness Monster didn't have a camera with them. But, there are a few pictures. The most famous one was taken in 1934. It shows an animal with a long neck and small head. In 1994, someone proved that this photograph was a trick. Two men made a model of the head. They put it on a toy submarine. They put the model in the lake. Then, they took the picture. It wasn't the only Loch Ness Monster trick. In 1933, huge footprints were found near the lake. It turned out that someone had made them with a stuffed hippo's foot!

Do a few tricks mean that the monster is a fake? Many people don't think so. Every year, dozens of people report that they have seen the famous animal. Scientists keep working to find proof. Then, we will know if there really is a monster in the deep, blue loch.

Monster in the Loch

Answer the questions below.

4. Finish the following sentence to tell about the trick picture that was taken in 1934.

   Two men made a _____

   of the head and put it on a _____

   _____ .

5. Besides the 1934 picture, which other Loch Ness Monster trick is described in the story?

   a. People made a fake film of the animal swimming.
   b. Somebody yelled that he could see the monster in the lake.
   c. Somebody made fake animal footprints near the lake.
   d. Two men made a model of the Loch Ness Monster.

6. Read the following sentence from the story and answer the question.

   Do a few tricks mean that the monster is a fake?

   Which of the following phrases could replace *is a fake*?

   a. is real
   b. isn't real
   c. is the truth
   d. is silly

7. When was the first written record of the Loch Ness Monster recorded?

   a. before 600 A.D.
   b. 1000 A.D.
   c. before 300 B.C.
   d. 100 A.D.

8. What did the Roman soldiers find when they came to Scotland?

   a. someone who showed them the monster
   b. a carving of a big, swimming animal
   c. a written record about the Loch Ness Monster
   d. b. and c.

9. Write three things that you think would prove the monster is real. Write your answers in complete sentences.

   a. _____

   _____

   b. _____

   _____

   c. _____

   _____

STOP

Where is Amelia?

Amelia Earhart was famous during her lifetime. She flew airplanes at a time when women didn't do things like that. She was the first woman to fly across the Atlantic Ocean. She made many daring trips. In 1937, Amelia planned another big trip. She planned to fly around the world. Instead, she vanished.

Most of her trip went well. She and her co-pilot got to the Pacific Ocean. On July 2, 1937, they planned to fly to a tiny island. A ship was nearby. It was there to listen for Amelia's messages on the radio.

The day was supposed to be clear. It was not. The flight took longer than planned. Amelia sent a message to the ship. She said her plane was getting low on gas. Then, she said she could not see the island. By that time, the plane had very little gas left. Amelia said she would keep sending messages. After that, there was only silence.

The President of the United States called for a search. Over $4 million was spent to try to find the lost pilot. Ships searched over 250,000 square miles of sea. The work lasted two weeks. No clues were found.

At first, people thought that the plane had just run out of gas. It must have crashed into the sea. Then, a reporter talked to Amelia's mother. She said that her daughter may have planned her trip for the government. Other people said Amelia was looking for facts about ships from Japan. Was Amelia Earhart a spy?

Make a prediction.

What do you think the author will write about next?

_____

Conversion

250,000 square miles = 647,497.03 square kilometers

Answer the following questions based on what you read on page 43. Then, finish reading the story at the bottom of the page.

1. The first part of the story describes all of the following EXCEPT—
   a. awards that Amelia Earhart won.
   b. Amelia's plan to fly around the world.
   c. why Amelia was famous.
   d. how much money was spent on the search for Amelia Earhart.

2. Which of the following is a synonym for *vanished*?
   a. valued
   b. disappeared
   c. ventured
   d. revisited

3. According to the story, what was one cause of Amelia's flight problems on July 2?
   a. She and her co-pilot were fighting.
   b. The radio didn't work on the plane.
   c. The island wasn't on the map.
   d. The weather was bad.

4. What is one adjective that describes Amelia Earhart?

   _____

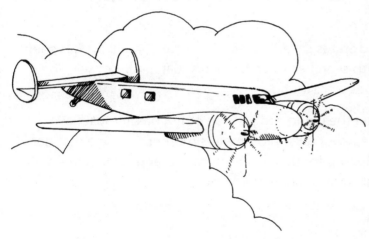

Four years later, the Japanese bombed Pearl Harbor. More stories were told about the brave pilot, Amelia Earhart. A movie was made. It showed a person like Amelia on a spy flight. After World War II, someone said that she had seen Amelia alive! She said that Amelia had been held by the Japanese. But, this story was never proved.

The search still goes on for Amelia Earhart. Many people have looked for her airplane. One person thought he had found her grave, but he had not. Other people have found parts of planes. They thought the parts were from the crash of Amelia's airplane. But, there was much fighting in the Pacific Ocean during World War II. There were many planes that crashed then.

No proof has ever been found about Amelia being a spy. Although, some people think that the huge search for her *was* spying! They think that the President asked for the big search so that he could find out more about Japanese ships. We may never know the whole story about this great pilot. She is gone, but her story lives on.

Next Page ➡

Where is Amelia?

Answer the questions below.

5. Which of the following sentences BEST summarizes the story?
   a. Since Amelia Earhart's plane vanished, there have been many theories about what happened.
   b. Since Amelia Earhart's plane vanished, it has been proven that she was arrested by the Japanese.
   c. Amelia Earhart was a famous pilot in her time, but no one really searches for her anymore.
   d. Amelia Earhart was on a spy flight for the President.

6. Read the following sentence from the story and answer the question.

   They think that the President asked for the big search so that he could find out more about Japanese ships.

   Why would the President want to know more about Japanese ships?
   a. He really liked ships.
   b. He wanted to build ships like the Japanese ships.
   c. The United States fought against the ships during World War II.
   d. He knew that Amelia Earhart liked ships.

7. What is a *spy*?
   a. an adviser to the President
   b. someone who looks for secrets from another government
   c. someone who goes on flights around the world
   d. none of the above

8. Which of the following is the BEST reason to think that Amelia Earhart might have been a spy?
   a. A movie hinted about it.
   b. The Japanese arrested Amelia.
   c. Her mother said Amelia may have been working for the government.
   d. Her plane was filled with secret information that she had found on her trip.

9. The author says some people believed—
   a. that the government may have used the search to spy on others.
   b. that the government spent too much money on the search.
   c. that the searchers found parts of the crashed plane.
   d. that the searchers spent too much time looking for the plane.

10. What do you think happened to Amelia Earhart? Write your answer in a complete sentence.

   _____

   _____

   _____

   _____

STOP

Lines in the Desert

Pretend you are flying over Peru. You look down from the plane's window. You can see long, straight lines and giant pictures from the air! The desert area, called the *pampa*, is covered with huge drawings. There is a spider. There is a monkey. There are big patterns. The pictures go on for miles. You have just seen the Nazca Lines.

The Nazca Lines were "drawn" on the desert over 1,000 years ago. The pampa is covered with small, black stones. There is yellow dirt under the stones. The lines were made by moving the stones so that the yellow dirt would show. The stones were piled beside the lines so that they made a small trench. The yellow lines stand out against the black stones. But, why make pictures that were so big? Some of the smaller pictures are the size of two American football fields. One of the longest lines is 40 miles long. And, what were these pictures for?

Some scientists think the pictures might be maps of constellations. When we look at the stars, we see a dipper, a hunter, and a bull. Maybe the people who made these pictures looked at the stars and saw a monkey, a bird, and a man who looked like an owl. Another idea is that the area was a place for religion. Pilgrims might have walked along the long, straight Nazca Lines to get from one religious place to another. The drawings might also be art.

It is the size of the pictures that puzzles people the most. On the ground, the lines are confusing. When you see them from an airplane, they make sense. The ancient people who made the pictures could not fly. Or, could they?

Make a prediction.

What do you think the author will write about next?

_____

_____

Conversion

40 miles = 64.37 kilometers

Next Page ➡

Answer the following questions based on what you read on page 46. Then, finish reading the story at the bottom of the page.

1.–5. Write T for true and F for false.

1. _____ The Nazca Lines are in Bolivia.

2. _____ Some of the lines make giant pictures in the desert.

3. _____ The Nazca Lines are over 1,000 years old.

4. _____ No one is sure why the Nazca Lines were made.

5. _____ One of the pictures in the desert is an owl.

6. Choose the word that BEST completes this sentence:

   The desert area where the Nazca Lines are found is called the _____.

   a. panama
   b. pampa
   c. pamper
   d. panpa

7. The first part of the story tells about all of the following EXCEPT—

   a. how the Nazca Lines were made.
   b. why some people think that the Nazca Lines might be pictures of constellations.
   c. how the Nazca Lines were discovered by explorers.
   d. how big the Nazca Lines are.

One American explorer, Jim Woodman, found pictures on an ancient Nazca pot. They seemed to be of a giant kite or hot-air balloon. Woodman wondered if the people who made the Nazca Lines had also learned how to fly. They found very tightly woven cloth in a tomb. Woodman and a friend made a triangle-shaped balloon like the one on the pottery. They used cloth like the kind that they found in the tomb. The balloon flew! So, maybe these ancient people did look at the Nazca Lines from the air. Or, maybe they could just picture the drawings from what they saw on the ground. We do know one thing—the Nazca Lines are one of the most interesting finds on Earth.

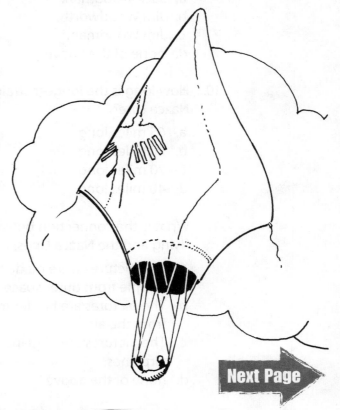

Next Page ➡

Name _____ Date _____

Lines in the Desert

Answer the questions below.

8. Read the following sentence from the story and answer the question.

   Some scientists think the pictures might be maps of constellations.

   What are *constellations*?
   a. groups of pictures
   b. groups of stars and planets
   c. maps of the layers of the atmosphere
   d. pictures made in the desert

9. The explorer who thought the ancient Nazca people could fly was—
   a. Jack Woodman.
   b. Jim Woodworth.
   c. Jim Woodman.
   d. none of the above

10. How long is the longest straight Nazca Line?
    a. 65 miles long
    b. 20 miles long
    c. 70 miles long
    d. 40 miles long

11. What is the connection between flying and the Nazca Lines?
    a. The pictures were made by people from outer space.
    b. The pictures are harder to see from the air.
    c. The pictures are of giant airplanes.
    d. none of the above

12. One of the Nazca Lines is a picture of a—
    a. toucan.
    b. bull.
    c. hunter.
    d. monkey.

13. Why do you think the pictures are still there after 1,000 years?
    a. The government has always kept people away from the lines.
    b. The pictures are in the desert where it doesn't rain, so they don't get washed away.
    c. The pictures have been repainted so that people can still enjoy them.
    d. The pictures are no longer there.

14. One theory about the Nazca Lines is that they were made to be used as

    _____

    _____ .

Conversions
65 miles = 104.61 kilometers
20 miles = 32.19 kilometers
70 miles = 112.65 kilometers
40 miles = 64.37 kilometers

A Ship without a Crew

It was 1872. Out at sea, Captain Morehouse of the *Dei Gratia* saw a ship that he knew. Out in the middle of the Atlantic Ocean, right in front of his ship, was the *Mary Celeste*. He knew the ship's captain, Benjamin Briggs. It looked like something was wrong. But, the *Mary Celeste* was not flying any flags that said the ship needed help. All of the ship's sails were up, but it was moving strangely. The *Dei Gratia* followed for two hours. Then, Captain Morehouse sent some of his crew over to the *Mary Celeste*. What they found scared them badly.

There was no one onboard! The *Mary Celeste* had become a ghost ship, sailing itself. There was no sign of the captain, his family, or anyone from the crew. The ship's cabin was wet. But, all of the cargo was fine. There was plenty of food and water. Why did all of the people on the *Mary Celeste* leave in the middle of the sea?

The crew of the *Dei Gratia* split into two groups. Half of them sailed on their own ship. The other half sailed the *Mary Celeste* to land. There, a judge looked at the ship. There were some strange clues. A compass had been smashed. All of the other tools needed to *navigate*, or direct, the ship were gone. All of the ship's papers were missing. A rope with a broken end was found hanging over the back of the ship. The lifeboat was missing.

Could the *Mary Celeste* have been robbed by pirates? No, because there was still money on the ship. All of the cargo was still there. Could the crew have risen up against the captain? There were no signs of blood on the ship. Sometimes when a crew took over a ship, the captain was sent away on the lifeboat. But, in this case, the crew was missing, too!

Make a prediction.

What do you think the author will write about next?

_____

Name_____ Date_____

**Answer the following questions based on what you read on page 49.
Then, finish reading the story at the bottom of the page.**

1. The captain of the *Dei Gratia* knew the captain of the _____ .

2. A smashed _____ was found onboard the *Mary Celeste*.

3. A _____ with one broken end was also found.

4. _____ was onboard the *Mary Celeste* when it was found.

5. List two things that were missing from the *Mary Celeste*.

   a. _____

   b. _____

The mystery of the *Mary Celeste* has raised many questions. There are also many theories about what happened to this strange ghost ship. One person claimed that he was a secret passenger on the *Mary Celeste*. He said that the captain dove into the sea to show that a man could swim with all of his clothes on. The crew crowded onto a new, little deck that had been built. The deck fell into the sea, and everyone was killed by sharks.

That strange story doesn't tell why the ship's papers and lifeboat were missing. Some people worried that the crew of the *Dei Gratia* had killed the people on the *Mary Celeste* to steal the cargo. Then, they made up the story about the ship sailing on its own. Some people think that the *Mary Celeste* was in a bad storm and filled with water. The captain told everyone to get into the lifeboat. They held on to the ship with the rope. Then, the rope snapped. The ship kept sailing away. The lifeboat sank in the storm. Another idea is that the captain thought there might be a fire onboard. That's why he told everyone to get into the lifeboat.

A ghost ship is scary to sailors. It reminds them of the things that can go wrong at sea. Maybe that's why the *Mary Celeste* has sailed from the sea into our imaginations.

Next Page

© Carson-Dellosa

A Ship without a Crew

Answer the questions below.

6. Read the following sentences from the story and answer the question.

One person claimed that he was a secret passenger on the *Mary Celeste*. He said that the captain dove into the sea to show that a man could swim with all of his clothes on.

Why does this seem like an untrue story?

a. A captain of a ship would not jump into the sea while a ship was moving.
b. Nobody who knew the sea would jump into the water.
c. If there had been a secret passenger, the crew of the *Dei Gratia* would have found him.
d. all of the above

7. The *Mary Celeste's* captain was—

a. Captain Morehouse.
b. Benjamin Britton.
c. Dei Gratia.
d. Benjamin Briggs.

8. Why did it seem unlikely that the *Mary Celeste* was robbed by pirates?

a. There was still money on the ship.
b. The pirates said they hadn't robbed the ship.
c. The cargo was still on the ship.
d. a. and c.

9. Which of the following theories is NOT discussed in the story?

a. The crew left the ship because there was too much water onboard.
b. The crew rose up against the captain.
c. The captain and crew were poisoned by bad food onboard.
d. Pirates robbed the ship.

10. What does *navigate* mean?

a. to predict
b. to sound out
c. to steer
d. none of the above

11. Which theory about the *Mary Celeste* do you think is true? Why do you think so? Write your answer in complete sentences.

_____

_____

_____

_____

_____

_____

Disappearing Act

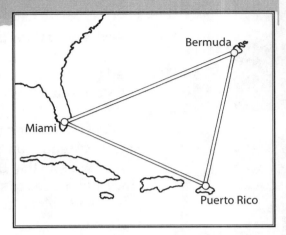

On a map, draw a line from Miami, Florida, to the island of Bermuda. Draw a second line from Bermuda to Puerto Rico, and a third line from Puerto Rico to Miami. This makes a triangle over the sea. Many people think that this area is one of the scariest places on Earth.

The triangle you have drawn is called the "Bermuda Triangle." Stories are told about strange things that happen there. Ships vanish. Planes lose their way. In 1815, a ship got lost in the triangle and made a war last longer. This ship was carrying the peace treaty to England to end the War of 1812. In 1945, a group of five airplanes flew into the triangle. The leader of the group lost his way. The group, called Flight 19, was never heard from again. There are many other stories of missing planes and ships.

Why is this part of the world so hard to navigate? There are many different ideas. Some think that *UFOs*, or unidentified flying objects, fly over the Bermuda Triangle. They think the UFOs pick up ships or airplanes. Then, they fly away. Some people say that the lost city of Atlantis is under the sea there. They think the city has a power that pulls ships and planes to it.

Those are stories that people like to tell. They are scary and interesting. But, are there realistic reasons that make the triangle a place of danger?

Make a prediction.

What do you think the author will write about next?

_____

© Carson-Dellosa

Answer the following questions based on what you read on page 52. Then, finish reading the story at the bottom of the page.

1. Many people think that the Bermuda Triangle is dangerous. Which of the following is NOT a possible reason that is discussed in the first part of the story?

   a. UFOs pick up ships and planes
   b. pirates capture ships and planes
   c. Atlantis pulls ships and planes under the water
   d. none of the above

2. The Bermuda Triangle is—

   a. found between Florida, Puerto Rico, and Bermuda.
   b. a place where many ships and planes are found.
   c. a safe place to learn how to sail.
   d. a triangle of sea near Japan.

3. The first part of the story describes all of the following about the Bermuda Triangle EXCEPT—

   a. where it is.
   b. why people are scared of it.
   c. what natural things might cause trouble there.
   d. examples of ships and planes that got lost there.

First of all, the Bermuda Triangle is a place that has many storms. These storms can form quickly. Sometimes, boaters and pilots get in trouble because of the sudden storms. Wind and rain make steering very hard. Also, many people who take boats out in this area are on vacation. They may not be good sailors. Some of them don't really know how to handle a boat. A boat in trouble can sink quickly.

The strangest thing about the Bermuda Triangle is linked to magnets. A compass is supposed to always point to *magnetic North*. But, not in the Bermuda Triangle. There, a compass points to *true North*. There is only one other place on Earth where this happens. It is in a sea near Japan. We don't know why compasses work differently in these two places. But, the difference can make it much easier to get lost . . . and then get into trouble.

Name _____ Date _____

Disappearing Act

Answer the questions below.

4. Look at the chain of events below and answer the question.

> A ship leaves for England in 1815 with a peace treaty.

↓

> The ship sails into the Bermuda Triangle.

↓

> The war lasts longer because the peace treaty does not arrive.

Which of the following events is missing from the sequence?

a. The ship gets lost sailing from Ireland to England.
b. There is a huge storm that delays the ship.
c. The ship vanishes in the Bermuda Triangle.
d. The ship is found in the Bermuda Triangle.

5. What is one realistic reason that a ship might get lost in the Bermuda Triangle?

a. Storms can happen very quickly there.
b. The water is very shallow in places.
c. Radios don't work there.
d. all of the above

6. Which of the following possible reasons for danger in the Bermuda Triangle is NOT realistic?

a. people on vacations sailing boats
b. differences in compass readings
c. power from the city of Atlantis
d. sudden storms

7. Read the following sentence from the story and answer the question.

Some of them don't really know how to handle a boat.

What is another way to say *handle a boat*?

a. sail a boat
b. control a boat
c. steer a boat
d. all of the above

8. Besides the Bermuda Triangle, the other place on Earth where compasses point to true North is—

a. the Arctic Ocean.
b. the sea near India.
c. the North Sea.
d. a sea near Japan.

The Lost City of Z

In 1906, an Englishman named Colonel Percy Fawcett went to Bolivia, a country in South America. It was his job to try to fill in a map of the country. Much of Bolivia is filled with mountains and rain forests. These places had not been explored yet. Fawcett was told that the job would be filled with danger. Travel was hard in Bolivia. There were many illnesses. And, the natives there were not friendly. Colonel Fawcett took the job anyway.

Fawcett faced many hardships as he worked to map the rain forest. He was bitten by vampire bats. He swam across rivers filled with man-eating fish. It was hard to hike in the rain forest. It was even harder to take a boat over the river rapids. For three years, the English colonel risked death every day.

After three years, his job was finished. But, Colonel Fawcett did not want to go home. He kept exploring on his own. This might seem like a strange choice. The colonel had a reason. He wanted to find the Lost City of Z.

Colonel Fawcett had heard many stories about this ancient city. He thought it might be in the rain forests of nearby Brazil. He spent almost 20 years trying to learn more about the ruins of this city. He wrote letters to his son, Brian, telling him what he heard about Z. Colonel Fawcett said that it was older than the pyramids in Egypt. He heard stories that the city was built of stone. It had low houses. It had a temple shaped like a pyramid. There were rumors that mines near the city were filled with gold. In 1926, Colonel Fawcett set out to find Z. He left on his trip with his other son, Jack. They were never seen again.

The Lost City of Z

Answer the following questions based on what you read on page 55. Then, finish reading the story on the next page.

1. The first part of the story is MOSTLY about—
   a. the people of Bolivia.
   b. Colonel Percy Fawcett and his explorations.
   c. Colonel Fawcett's son, Brian.
   d. the Lost City of Z.

2. Where is Bolivia?
   a. South America
   b. Mexico
   c. Central America
   d. none of the above

3. Why did Colonel Fawcett stay in Bolivia after his job was finished?
   a. He wanted to learn a new language.
   b. He wanted to go river rafting.
   c. He wanted to find an ancient, lost city.
   d. He wanted to build a new home for his sons.

4. What did people say the Lost City of Z looked like?
   a. It had tall stone buildings and a round temple.
   b. It had a temple shaped like a pyramid and low buildings.
   c. It had gold mines nearby.
   d. b. and c.

5. What was the reason that Colonel Fawcett FIRST went to Bolivia?
   a. to find rubber trees for a British company
   b. to help map the unexplored places in Bolivia
   c. to find the Lost City of Z
   d. to find gold mines for his family

6. Read the following sentence from the story and answer the question.

   Fawcett faced many hardships as he worked to map the rain forest.

   What is a synonym for *hardships*?
   a. lightships
   b. differences
   c. troubles
   d. prospects

7. What do you think the author will write about next? Write your answer in complete sentences.

   _____

   _____

   _____

   _____

   _____

Next Page ▶

**Finish reading "The Lost City of Z" below.
Then, answer the questions on page 58.**

What happened to Colonel Fawcett? Did he die in the rain forests of Brazil? Did he and Jack ever find Z? The colonel told his wife that if he did not come back, she should not send a search party for him and his son. There were too many dangers. But, search parties did try. Even 70 years later, a team tried to go into the rain forest to trace the steps of Colonel Fawcett. They were stopped by angry members of a native tribe. The tribe kept them for three days before letting them go. So, maybe the colonel was right about the danger!

Other people said they saw the colonel, and he was still alive. He was being held by natives in the rain forest. Still other people thought that he made it to the Lost City of Z. They said he loved it so much that he just stayed there. The mines of Z held great riches. Maybe the colonel became a king in the rain forest.

Colonel Fawcett's son, Brian, searched twice to try to find his father and his brother. In 1952, Brian flew over part of the rain forests of Brazil. This was where he thought his father had gone. From the plane, he saw a group of huge limestone piles. These were not buildings. They were natural groups of rocks. The limestone had eroded in the rain and sun. Brian said they looked just like an ancient city. It made him sad to think that this might have been the "city" that his father heard stories about. Had Colonel Fawcett risked his life for nothing?

Even today, the rain forests of Bolivia and Brazil hide many secrets. People still find it hard to travel to these places. Maybe someday, people will learn more about Colonel Fawcett's last trip. And, maybe someday, an explorer can really retrace his steps to see if the Lost City of Z is real.

Next Page

Name _____ Date _____

The Lost City of Z

Answer the questions below.

8. Look at the chain of events below and answer the question.

> Colonel Fawcett helps map parts of Bolivia.

↓

> The colonel hears stories about an ancient lost city.

↓

> The colonel stays in South America to learn more about the lost city.

↓

> The colonel's son, Brian, goes to Brazil to look for his father and brother.

Which step is missing?
a. Colonel Fawcett is attacked by bats.
b. Brian Fawcett travels with his father in Bolivia and Brazil.
c. Brian Fawcett flies over Brazil.
d. Colonel Fawcett and Jack Fawcett disappear while trying to find the lost city.

9. Which of the following problems of rain forest exploration is NOT mentioned in the story?
a. river rapids
b. illness
c. snakes
d. vampire bats

10. Read the following sentence from the story and answer the question.

The limestone had eroded in the rain and sun.

What does *eroded* mean?
a. worn down
b. erased
c. vanished
d. melted

11. Why did Brian Fawcett think that the stories his father heard about a lost city were not true?
a. The city was in Brazil.
b. He saw giant rock piles that looked like a city.
c. Other people who had seen the rocks might have told his father about them.
d. b. and c.

12. In what year did Colonel Fawcett first go to South America?
a. 1926
b. 1952
c. 1906
d. 1916

58 CD-104179 ■ Strange and Unexplained

© Carson-Dellosa

A Circle of Stones

On the plain of Salisbury in England is a strange and mysterious sight. A ring of giant stones sits in the middle of the plain. There are no other large stones or boulders in sight. Some of the stones in the ring are stacked on top of others. Who made this strange circle? What is it for?

Those two questions have been debated for centuries. For a long time, people thought that ancient priests of the Druids had made the strange circle. We now know that this is not true. The Druids followed a religion based on gods of nature. But, they did not start their religion in England until about 300 B.C. That was more than 1,500 years after *Stonehenge*, the stone circle, was built.

The Romans lived in England for a time. They were great builders. Did they build Stonehenge? No, they did not. The Romans came to England in 100 B.C. They wrote about the stone circle in their reports. The Romans thought that the Druids used the ring as some kind of *temple*, or church. But, they were not sure. By that time, it seems that no one was using the strange ring of stones.

All we know for sure is what Stonehenge was *not* used for! Scientists have not found groups of bodies buried inside the ring, so it wasn't a grave. There are no bones from feasts, so it wasn't a place for parties. There are no weapons buried there, so it wasn't a place to prepare for war.

Next Page

A Circle of Stones

Answer the following questions based on what you read on page 59. Then, finish reading the story on the next page.

1. Which of the following sentences is the BEST summary of the first part of the story?
   a. Stonehenge was a Druid temple.
   b. Stonehenge is a mysterious circle of stones in England; its purpose is not known.
   c. Stonehenge was built on the plain of Salisbury by the Romans.
   d. Stonehenge was built around 100 B.C.

2. Who were the *Druids*?
   a. ancient priests
   b. people who worshipped nature
   c. Roman priests
   d. the people who built Stonehenge

3. What is a *temple*?
   a. a type of church
   b. a type of school
   c. a ring of stones
   d. a Roman plaza

4. The first part of the story says that we know Stonehenge was NOT used for—
   a. talking to the dead.
   b. viewing the stars.
   c. preparing for battles.
   d. all of the above

5.–9. Write T for true or F for false.

5. _____ The Romans came to England in about 300 B.C.

6. _____ Stonehenge was not used as a grave.

7. _____ We know that feasts were held inside the stone circle of Stonehenge.

8. _____ Stonehenge was not a place to prepare for war.

9. _____ The Romans wrote about Stonehenge in their reports.

10. What do you think the author will write about next? Write your answer in complete sentences.

   _____

   _____

   _____

   _____

   _____

   _____

Next Page

**Finish reading "A Circle of Stones" below.
Then, answer the questions on page 62.**

Stonehenge is built so that it lines up with the sun on the longest and shortest days of the year. Was it some kind of giant calendar? Near Stonehenge are many *burial mounds*, the graves of important leaders from the same time. Was Stonehenge built to honor these leaders? Was it a place where priests talked to the dead? There are many theories about the giant stone ring. But, what is more amazing is that Stonehenge was built at all.

Stonehenge was built over a period of hundreds of years. The first Stonehenge had no stones. It was marked with a ditch that circled around a ring of *pits*, or holes in the ground. Some scientists think that wooden posts stood in the holes. They might have been like totem poles.

Five hundred years later, the first stones were put in the ring. These are called the Blue Stones. They weigh four tons each. They were somehow dragged to Stonehenge from mountains that are over 200 miles away!

Over the next 1,000 years, even larger "standing stones" were put in the ring. Each pair of these stones supports another stone like a roof. Scientists are still arguing about how these enormous stones were moved and pulled into a standing position. The heaviest of the stones weighs over 40 tons. Long ago, people thought that they were put in place by magic. Today, we still do not know for sure how Stonehenge was built.

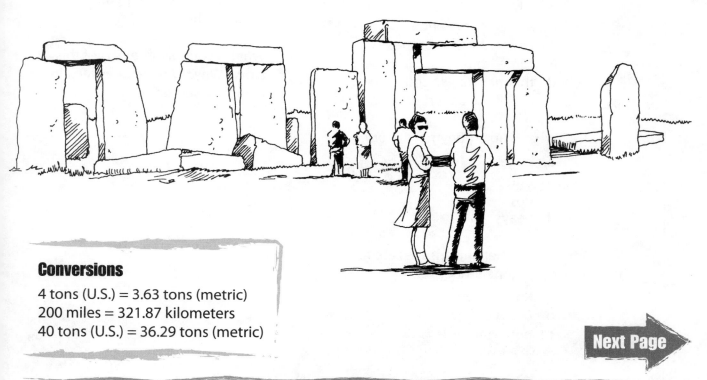

Conversions

4 tons (U.S.) = 3.63 tons (metric)
200 miles = 321.87 kilometers
40 tons (U.S.) = 36.29 tons (metric)

Next Page

A Circle of Stones

Answer the questions below.

11. Read the following sentences from the story and answer the question.

   Some scientists think that wood posts stood in the holes. They might have been like totem poles.

   What is a *totem pole*?

   a. a type of lumber
   b. a type of tree
   c. a carved, wooden pole to honor ancestors
   d. a cane or staff used by a priest

12. The story talks about all of the following things EXCEPT—

   a. experiments that were done to try to move stones like the ones at Stonehenge.
   b. what the Romans thought about Stonehenge.
   c. where the Blue Stones came from.
   d. theories that scientists have about the uses of Stonehenge.

13. What is an antonym for *enormous*?

   a. huge
   b. bulky
   c. tiny
   d. heavy

14. What other ancient sites are found near Stonehenge?

   a. Roman houses
   b. Druid villages
   c. burial mounds
   d. a. and c.

15. From details in the story, we know that Stonehenge was built—

   a. around 300 B.C.
   b. before 1800 B.C.
   c. after 100 B.C.
   d. around 200 A.D.

16. Based on the information in the story, what can you infer about Stonehenge?

   a. It was probably built by ancient people that we don't know much about.
   b. It might have been built as a large calendar or a place to view the sun.
   c. It was built with skills that amaze us because moving the stones was so difficult.
   d. all of the above

17. What is your favorite part of this story? Why? Write your answer in complete sentences.

   _____

   _____

   _____

   _____

   _____

STOP

Answer Key

Page 6
1. b. 2. c.
3. ice bombs, street, Spain
4. a. 5. c.
6. chemicals
7. huge, sudden, mysterious

Page 8
1. c. 2. b. 3. a.
4. Some people thought that it was too easy for subjects to cheat.
5. five
6. send
7. picture
8. b.

Page 10
1. d.
2. The Marfa lights are named for the town of Marfa, Texas.
3. a. 4. F 5. T 6. T
7. T 8. T 9. c.
10. lights from boats

Page 12
1. c. 2. d.
3. Woolpit
4. One
5. tunnel
6. English
7. d. 8. d.
9. Answers will vary.

Page 14
1. A yeti is a wild, furry man who lives in the mountains.
2. c. 3. T 4. F
5. F 6. T 7. F
8. b. 9. d. 10. b.

Page 16
1. c. 2. d. 3. c.
4. a. 5. a.
6. Answers will vary.

Page 18
1. a. 2. c. 3. b.
4. c. 5. a. 6. b.
7. Answers will vary.

Page 20
1. c. 2. e. 3. a. 4. b.
5. d. 6. d. 7. b.
8. missing link
9. Dan Gebo
10. ancestor
11. c.
12. Answers will vary.

Page 22
1. Huan
2. the black bear or the mountain lion
3. giant tortoise
4. Arizona
5. d. 6. c. 7. d.
8. Answers will vary but may include:
   a. One animal likes the scent of another animal.
   b. One animal is lonely or has lost a baby.
   c. One animal has to trust the other in order for it to survive.

Page 24
1. b. 2. a. 3. d.
4. c. 5. c.
6. Answers will vary.

Page 26
1. c. 2. c. 3. a.
4. c. 5. F 6. T
7. F 8. F 9. d.

Page 28
1. d. 2. b. 3. b. 4. c.
5. staff
6. eighth (or eight)
7. Answers will vary.

Page 30
1. b. 2. c. 3. c. 4. a.
5. Circle Makers
6. Answers will vary but may include:
   a. Crop circles might be made by people as works of art.
   b. Crop circles might be made by UFOs.
   c. Crop circles might be made by strange weather patterns.

Page 31
theories about Flores Man

Page 32
1. c. 2. d.
3. Flores Man is a race of tiny people that was discovered on the island of Flores in the Pacific Ocean.
4. tiny, hunter, mysterious

Page 33
5. c. 6. a. 7. c.
8. d. 9. c. 10. c.

Next Page

Page 34
more about Walz and whether he finds the mine

Page 35
1. c.   2. c.   3. c.

Page 36
4. F   5. T   6. T   7. F
8. b.   9. a.   10. c.
11. Answers will vary.

Page 37
other finds in the pit

Page 38
1. Daniel McGinnis
2. 30 feet
3. Canada
4. pirates
5. c.   6. a.

Page 39
7. b.   8. a.   9. d.   10. b.
11. Answers will vary.

Page 40
tricks that lead some people to think the monster cannot be real

Page 41
1. d.   2. d.
3. Answers will vary but may include:
   a. as big as a bus
   b. a swimming animal (like a seal)
   c. looks like a dinosaur (small head, long neck)

Page 42
4. model, toy submarine
5. c.   6. b.   7. a.   8. b.
9. Answers will vary.

Page 43
theories about why some people thought Earhart was a spy

Page 44
1. a.   2. b.   3. d.
4. Answers will vary but may include: brave, talented, famous, courageous

Page 45
5. a.   6. c.   7. b.
8. c.   9. a.
10. Answers will vary.

Page 46
ancient people and the possibility of flight

Page 47
1. F   2. T   3. T   4. T
5. F   6. b.   7. c.

Page 48
8. b.   9. c.   10. d.
11. d.   12. d.   13. b.
14. Answers will vary but may include: maps of constellations, religious places, art

Page 49
what happened to the people on the ship or theories about what happened to them

Page 50
1. *Mary Celeste*
2. compass
3. rope
4. No one
5. Answers will vary but should include two of the following: the lifeboat, the crew, navigation tools, the ship's papers

Page 51
6. d.   7. d.   8. d.
9. c.   10. c.
11. Answers will vary.

Page 52
possible realistic reasons that the Bermuda Triangle is dangerous

Page 53
1. b.   2. a.   3. c.

Page 54
4. c.   5. a.   6. c.
7. d.   8. d.

Page 56
1. b.   2. a.   3. c.
4. d.   5. b.   6. c.
7. Answers will vary but may include: The author is going to discuss theories about what happened to Colonel Fawcett and his son, Jack.

Page 58
8. d.   9. c.   10. a.
11. d.   12. c.

Page 60
1. b.   2. b.   3. a.
4. c.   5. F   6. T
7. F   8. T   9. T
10. Answers will vary but may include: The story will discuss possible uses or reasons for Stonehenge.

Page 62
11. c.   12. a.   13. c.   14. c.
15. b.   16. d.
17. Answers will vary.

STOP